# DODD, MEAD WONDERLAND BOOKS

*Banff, Alberta, as seen from the popular gondola lift. Thousands come here annually to fish the streams, ride the mountain trails, attend the school of fine arts, swim in the hot springs, or just enjoy the breathtaking scenery of the Canadian Rockies.*

# CANADA
## Wonderland of Surprises

### MAX BRAITHWAITE

ILLUSTRATED WITH PHOTOGRAPHS AND MAPS

DODD, MEAD & COMPANY, NEW YORK

*Opposite: The Citadel of Quebec City, perched above the St. Lawrence, where Wolfe defeated Montcalm in 1759.*

**For my wife, Aileen, who helped me with this book**

## ACKNOWLEDGMENTS

Thanks to the Canadian Government Travel Bureau, Alberta Department of Industry and Development, Ontario Department of Tourism and Information, Saskatchewan Government Photo Service, Manitoba Department of Industry and Commerce, Province of Quebec Film Bureau, British Columbia Department of Recreation and Conservation, Nova Scotia Information Service, New Brunswick Travel Bureau, Prince Edward Island Department of Travel and Publicity, Newfoundland Tourist Development Office and the National Film Board for their generous co-operation in supplying pictures for this book.

## CREDITS FOR PHOTOGRAPHS

Alberta Government Photograph. Department of Industry and Development, Edmonton, Alta, 9, 46; British Columbia Government Photograph. Department of Recreation and Conservation, Victoria, BC., 18; Canadian Government Travel Bureau, Ottawa, 2, 6, 12, 13, 16, 17, 27, 31, 37, 40, 43, 44, 47, 51, 53, 62; Manitoba Department of Industry and Commerce, 35; Ontario Department of Tourism and Publicity, 41; Province of Quebec Film Bureau, 5, 23; Saskatchewan Government Photo, 26.

Special appreciation goes to the Canadian Government Travel Bureau and to the Canadian Pacific for making it possible to use the lovely color photographs on the jacket of this book.

# Contents

The changing of the Guard in the nation's capital, Ottawa, Canada, follows the centuries-old tradition of Buckingham Palace, in England, with the precise pageantry of the Guards in their bearskin hats and scarlet tunics and the stirring military music.

# I

# Misconceptions and Facts

Most people, when asked where Canada is, will reply: "North of the United States." But this isn't entirely true. Windsor, Ontario, one of Canada's leading industrial cities, is farther south than such familiar places in the United States as Seattle, Washington; Portland, Maine; Minneapolis, Minnesota; Milwaukee, Wisconsin; Detroit, Michigan; Buffalo, Rochester, and Syracuse in New York State, and even Boston, Massachusetts. Canada actually extends farther south than nine American states, not counting Alaska. Most surprising of all is the fact that the farthest south region of Canada, Pelee Island in Lake Erie, is actually farther south than the northern border of California.

Canada is full of such surprises, and of paradoxes. Sports-loving summer visitors to Canada carry skis on the top of their cars, only to discover that the region of the country where they are visiting is hotter than it is at home. And yet, in parts of Canada there is skiing all year round. Others come hoping to snap a picture of a Mountie on horseback and probably never see one. But, if they exceed the speed limit on one of Canada's excellent highways, they can be stopped by a Mountie in a high-powered cruiser. Still others may have the idea that all Canadians speak French, but during their entire stay may never hear the language, although there are thousands of Canadians who speak no other.

Many think of Canada as "great open spaces for hunting and fishing." Then they visit Toronto and see nothing but skyscrapers, thousands of factories, freeways, traffic jams, and suburbs stretching for miles in all directions. Yet millions of square miles of Canada do contain nothing but wild life and a few native hunters.

Young people come expecting to see Eskimos or Indians but, instead, see other young people who dress, talk, and look exactly as they do—and sing the same songs, watch the same movies, read the same comic strips, drive the same makes of cars, drink the same brands of pop, and scream over the same singing groups.

The reasons for these misconceptions lie in the fact that Canada is an immense country (second largest in the world) and a country of great diversity of land forms, climate, and people. At the same time, it is sparsely populated, containing in its whole vast area only slightly more people than are found in New York State. And most of these people live along a narrow strip just north of the southern border, all within a few hours' motoring distance of the United States. The people in Saint John's, Newfoundland, are actually closer to Ireland than they are to their countrymen across the North American continent in Vancouver. And nearly all Canadians live closer to Americans than to their fellow Canadians in other provinces.

To gain any understanding of this broad, diverse country it is first of all necessary to know a few basic facts:

— Canada is a wide country, extending farther west than any part of the United States except Alaska, and more than six hundred miles farther east than Maine. Northward, Canada extends to within five hundred miles of the North Pole.

— Canada is an immensely rich country, possessing tremendous amounts of minerals, great forests, millions of acres of fertile farm land and, perhaps most important of all, more fresh water in its lakes and rivers than is found in any other country on earth.

— Canada is a young country, being about the same age as its close neighbor, the United States, and having many of the same problems. But . . .

— Canada is a British country. And this makes a difference. Like Australia, India, Great Britain, and others, she is a member of the British Commonwealth of Nations. At the same time, Canada is a democracy whose people are in full charge of their government.

— Canada is a beautiful country. The breathtaking splendor of the Rockies has been compared to that of the Alps. The color spectrum of eastern Canada's autumn leaves matches that of Vermont and New Hampshire. The northern lights, the prairie sunsets, and the midnight sun all have their spectacular uniqueness.

— With the exception of its west coast, Canada has a harsh, inhospita-

*Maligne Lake in Jasper National Park. Millions of acres of unspoiled land have been set aside as National Parks for the enjoyment of Canadians and their guests.*

ble climate, bitterly cold in winter, hot and humid in summer, and frightfully windy most of the time. Whereas in many countries physical life is easy, in Canada, for the most part, it is brutally hard.

All of these factors have their effect on the work, recreation, character, and attitudes of Canadians.

# 2

# The Big Country

Canada has only one close neighbor, the United States. But it borders on three of the world's major oceans, the Pacific, the Atlantic, and the Arctic. Excellent harbors on the east and west coasts have made Canada a great shipping nation, supplying farm, forest, and mineral products, as well as furs, fish, and manufactured goods to many countries of the world.

Canada is in the North Temperate Zone and, since most of the country lies in the path of the prevailing westerly winds, there is a saying that "All weather comes from the west." And because of the immense size of the country, there is a great variety of weather conditions. Trappers in the Yukon have felt it as cold as 81 degrees below zero, and at that temperature engine oil becomes hard as tar and lungs will freeze in minutes. However, Southern Alberta cowboys have had to cope with Death Valley-like temperatures of 115 degrees above zero.

Precipitation is equally varied. At Ocean Falls, on the west coast, where the high mountains rob ocean winds of moisture, the average annual precipitation is a soggy 175 inches. Critics of the beautiful west coast city of Vancouver complain that "it rains all the time." In the interior of British Columbia, however, at Kelowna, for instance, fruit growers have to manage with only twelve inches of moisture a year.

The prairies are dry and Eastern Canada has moderate rainfall. The only consistent thing you can say about Canadian weather is that it is inconsistent. You never know what to expect. Some winters are mild; others terribly cold. There may be frost every month of the summer or it may be blazing hot. It is frequently warmer in Whitehorse than in Toronto. In one day, the temperature can vary by 50 degrees and the difference between winter lows and summer highs can be 150 degrees or even more.

To understand the land forms and resources of the country, we must know what happened to North America before man made his appearance. At least four times—400 million years ago, 290 million years ago, 250 million years ago, and 100 million years ago—shallow seas covered much of the interior of the continent. Through the millions of years calcium and hydrocarbons from the bodies of billions of sea creatures created limestone and petroleum. Then four times in the last million years the whole area of Canada (and part of the United States) was covered with mile-deep layers of ice that depressed the land, bulldozed it into ridges and hills (eskers and moraines), and, on melting, filled the depressions with water to give Canada its hundreds of thousands of lakes. Mountains heaved and weathered away and heaved again in other places. Great glacial lakes dried to make tremendous fertile plains. Thus Canada was formed.

So, today, there is not one Canada—in a geographic sense—there are

11

a number of Canadas. We will consider them as the early settlers found them—from east to west.

The east coast of Canada is extremely irregular, with innumerable inlets (drowned valleys) stretching deep into the land and making excellent harbors for fishing boats and cargo ships. The Maritime Provinces (Newfoundland and Labrador, Prince Edward Island, Nova Scotia, and New Brunswick) all look to the Atlantic for their prosperity.

The Basque fishermen who came to this coast (some of them, it is believed, before Columbus reached America) found such an abundance of codfish as to impede the progress of ships. Sailors caught them by dropping a basket over the side of their craft. For hundreds of years dried salt cod was the principal export of the region. Cod is still king. The Newfoundlanders, particularly, catch these big fish with their jigging lines, long liners, and huge draggers. Lobsters, too, and many other varieties of sea life are still important to the Maritimers.

The terrain of the Maritime Provinces is mostly the ancient Appalachian Highlands that are found in the eastern part of the United States. On the hillsides and in the valleys between are great forests, providing pulpwood and lumber for export. There is relatively little good

*Through the Narrows, into the natural harbor of St. John's, Newfoundland, fishing boats have come for centuries. The capital of Canada's youngest province, it is the furthest east city in North America.*

*The Welland Canal is part of the St. Lawrence Seaway System which allows ocean vessels to sail far inland by a series of eight great locks.*

farm land, but potatoes thrive to the extent that they form the principal crop of Prince Edward Island and New Brunswick. From the sheltered Annapolis Valley of Nova Scotia thousands of tons of apples are shipped to the United States and Britain.

The streams are still rich in Atlantic salmon, and moose, deer, and bear attract hunters from all parts of the North American continent.

Under the land lie valuable stores of coal, iron ore, silver, zinc, lead, and tungsten.

The numerous rivers that tumble from the interior highlands to the ocean provide water power to run pulp mills, smelters, and factories.

Because of the frigid Labrador Current that, in season, brings Arctic pack ice into the harbors, the climate is wet, cold, and windy. But there are enough fine days which, along with the beautiful scenery, make the Maritime Provinces a favorite vacation land.

The Saint Lawrence River and the Great Lakes are nature's greatest gift to Canada. By the river the early explorers found their way into the heart of the continent. Today, through the miraculous system of dams and locks of the International Seaway, ocean-going ships from all over the world find their way up the Saint Lawrence, across the Great Lakes to Toronto, Hamilton, Windsor, and as far inland as Port Arthur and Fort William at the western tip of Lake Superior. The Seaway is undoubtedly the greatest inland navigation system in the world.

The area of the Saint Lawrence–Great Lakes Lowlands is blessed in other ways. Niagara Falls has long provided the power to help make southern Ontario the manufacturing center of Canada. The rivers flowing into the Saint Lawrence from the highlands to the north generate the power for Montreal's great manufacturing industries.

The land between the lakes is flat, fertile, and well watered, providing for all kinds of agriculture. And in the southern peninsula of Ontario are grown many crops not usually associated with Canada. The famous Ontario blue grapes flourish in the Niagara peninsula between Lakes Erie and Ontario, along with peaches, pears, cherries, and other fruits. On the flat, sandy land north of Lake Erie are hundreds of large, prosperous tobacco farms.

Around the small town of Petrolia, not far from the tip of Lake Huron, the first petroleum wells of Canada (perhaps of North America) were drilled, and here the early petroleum industry developed. Today, the famous "Chemical Valley," with Sarnia as its center, is the largest oil-refining area of Canada.

The climate is kinder in southern Ontario than in any other part of Canada (except for the west coast), and here more than one-quarter of all Canadians make their home.

On any Friday afternoon and evening in summer the roads leading north from Toronto and other southern Ontario cities are choked with cars. Many are towing boats with high-powered motors attached. And inside these cars the young people are polishing water skis, fondling fishing rods, and thinking of plunges from high rocks into deep, clear blue water.

They are going north to the vacation lands of central Canada. That is the southern tip of the Canadian Shield, a vast, V-shaped area around Hudson Bay, covering all of Northern Ontario, Northern Quebec, the northern parts of the Prairie Provinces, and most of the Arctic—in all about half of Canada. It is rock country. Precambrian rock, the oldest and hardest on the earth's surface, sticks up in smooth or jagged mounds. A thin layer of soil supports great forests.

And in all the depressions of the rocks are the crystal-clear lakes, large and small. So numerous are these that, when you look down from an aircraft on this area, you see far more water than land.

It is impossible to exaggerate the beauty of these vacation lands. In summertime there are the varying shades of green of the pine, spruce, birch, poplar, oak, and maple trees. In the fall, the deciduous trees turn gold and red and shimmering yellow among the evergreens. In winter, bare tree trunks cast long, grotesque shadows on the knee-deep, pure-white snow. The Laurentian Highlands north of Montreal are the delight of thousands of skiers.

When you travel farther north and west on the Shield, you are in mining country. Gold mines, copper mines, and the largest nickel mines in the world have been found in the wilderness, and around them have grown up the cities of Sudbury, Noranda, Elliott Lake, Flin Flon, Thompson, and many others.

Modern transportation and techniques have opened previously inaccessible areas to man's use. In Labrador, near the Quebec border, hundreds of miles from civilization, we find the city of Wabush, as modern as any Los Angeles or London suburb, with brand-new houses, municipal offices, schools, churches, community center, even green lawns. Here live engineers from Toronto and Dallas, Texas; miners from Newfoundland and Quebec, learning each other's language. There are people who came from Europe, too. And it's all because of an immense mountain of iron ore nearby which for years will feed the hungry blast furnaces of Pittsburgh, Pennsylvania; Gary, Indiana; Hamilton, Ontario, and elsewhere.

Pulp and paper mills dot the Canadian Shield in northern Quebec and Ontario, providing millions of tons of paper for the presses of the world.

Shortly after you cross the border from Ontario into southern Manitoba you are aware of an abrupt change of scenery. You can see for miles! No more rocks, no more trees—just the flat, flat prairie stretching endlessly to the horizon and the oh-so-big sky.

*Grain crops and summer fallow create a giant checkerboard on the flat land of Regina Plain.*

This is the Great Central Plain of Canada, with its millions of acres of the best grain-growing land in the world. It covers most of the southern portions of Manitoba, Saskatchewan, and Alberta, known as Canada's Prairie Provinces. This area is also called "the bread basket of the world." Each year, upward of 800 million bushels of wheat are harvested from the immense farms and shipped in long freight trains to the head of Lake Superior. From there they journey through the Seaway to the Atlantic and so to the hungry countries of Europe and Asia.

In the drier, southwestern portions of the Plains are the great rolling ranch lands where cowboys round up the white-faced cattle for shipment to the East.

And all across the Plains the traveler is surprised to see small black pumps working away in wheat field and pasture. This is because under the Plains are riches equal to those on the surface. In 1947, after years of trying, oil drillers at Leduc, Alberta, twenty miles south of Edmonton, brought in a gusher. It was the beginning of a petroleum development that extends over the three provinces, and has turned Canada from an importer of oil to a large exporter. Natural gas in almost unlimited quantities was also found, and now pipe lines carry the precious fuel across the land to heat the houses, run the factories, and power cars and farm machinery of the country.

16

While probing for oil in Saskatchewan, drillers continually brought up white salt which turned out to be potash, a much-needed ingredient of fertilizers. Further exploration showed that the potash beds extended right across southern Saskatchewan and into Manitoba. Now potash is shipped from more than half a dozen Prairie mines at the rate of millions of tons a year.

Water is scarce on the Prairies, as it is in the American Southwest. To counteract this, the wide, swift-flowing Saskatchewan River has been dammed at Outlook, providing a four-hundred-mile-long lake, with water for recreation, irrigation, and hydroelectric power.

When driving westward from the city of Calgary, the traveler is struck by a line of jagged, snow-covered peaks looming on the horizon. As he moves on through the foothills, they loom larger and larger, with

*The Trans Canada Highway, which took many years to build, has done more than anything since the railroad to unite Canadians. Here the highway and the railroad wind through a six-mile gorge in Glacier National Park, British Columbia.*

breathtaking beauty. Before long, he is in the famous Canadian Rockies, part of the immense Cordillera region that covers the western side of North America from Alaska to Panama.

Soon the great towering chunks of granite and limestone are all about, with the highway a narrow, winding ribbon between. Unlike the American Rockies, the Canadian Rockies present an almost solid wall, extending from the Arctic Ocean to the United States border. Automobiles and trains can traverse them only through a few high passes with colorful names such as Kicking Horse Pass and Crowsnest Pass.

The mountain ranges with their deep valleys between contain riches beyond belief. Great forests of spruce and pine cover the mountain slopes. Immense lakes fill the valleys. And in the hard rock of the mountains are copper, zinc, lead, gold, and other minerals, waiting to be taken.

On the high, flat plateau in the center of British Columbia is located the ranching country known as "The Cariboo." Here immense herds are driven to the high country and back to the plain, as grazing conditions demand.

The Trans-Canada Highway and the railways follow the roaring

*High-rise apartments overlooking English Bay, in Vancouver. Each is planned to give the best possible view of the Pacific Ocean.*

Fraser River south through the middle Cordillera. At the city of Hope, not far north of the American border, the river makes a right-angle turn to the west and flows placidly to the sea. Over thousands of years, silt carried by the river has formed a fertile plain on which flourish orchards, market gardens, and dairy cattle. The Fraser flows into the Pacific Ocean at Vancouver.

The Pacific coast of Canada is noted for four things—it has heavy rainfall; it has deep fiords extending like long, bent fingers in among the mountains; the Japanese Current warms the land; and there is a large island off the coast known as Vancouver Island.

In the bordering sea, salmon are caught by the millions. These are canned in huge plants and shipped abroad.

On the wet west slopes of the mountains grow the giant Douglas fir and red cedar, two of the finest lumber trees on the North American continent. Every harbor along the coast is filled with rafts of their logs being floated southward to the sawmills of Vancouver.

With its excellent port, abundance of raw materials, and hydro-electric power developed from mountain rivers, Vancouver is fast becoming a leading manufacturing center.

If you look at the map of Canada in this book you will note that a large portion of the country lies north of the 60th parallel of latitude. This is usually referred to as "The North." It is a vast area, comprising more than a million and a half square miles (39 per cent of Canada), but containing only about forty thousand people, approximately the same number as live in a small city.

Since it is so vast, the North has many different land forms. In the west are the Cordilleras, then a narrow extension of the plain on either side of the Mackenzie River, and east of that the Canadian Shield. Much of the eastern Arctic is treeless tundra, and the islands to the north are covered with ice the year round.

Two of North America's biggest lakes, Great Slave Lake and Great Bear, are part of the Mackenzie River system, and there are numerous other lakes and rivers draining into the Arctic Ocean.

Polar bear, seal, walrus, beluga whale, and the curious narwhale with a horn in the middle of his forehead live in the Arctic waters. On land, caribou and muskox miraculously survive on the tiny lichens and

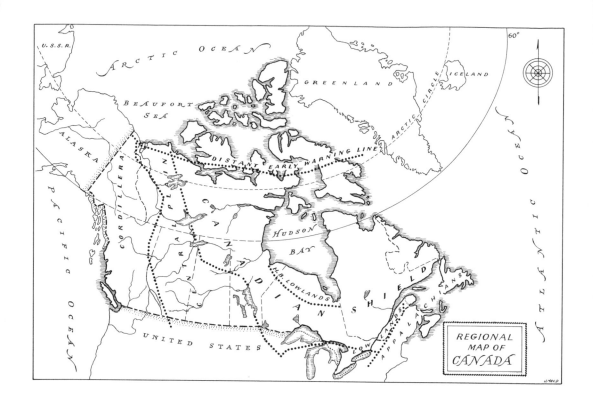

reindeer moss. Wolves, white fox, barren land grizzly, and weasels prey on the Arctic hare, lemmings, voles, and mice that thrive by the millions. Geese, ducks, swans, terns, and dozens of other birds make the long trip to the Arctic every summer to build their nests and raise their young. And during the short growing season, hundreds of small colorful plants such as the Arctic poppy and the bluebell cover the ground. In the long, dark, cold winter shrieking blizzards bury all with drifting snow.

Until recently, the North has been too cold and too remote to entice settlers. Only about 10,000 Eskimos and 7,000 Indians were scattered over the whole area, living by hunting and trapping. But, as new resources are discovered, as transportation and communication have developed, and as men have learned to control their environment, the sleeping North has sprung to life. In Chapter 4 we will see how this has affected the lives of the people there.

# 3

# Long Story of a Young Country

In 1961, the Norwegian archaeologist, Helege Ingstad, digging at L'Anse aux Meadows, at the northern tip of Newfoundland, made an important discovery. It was the remains of a Norse dwelling and furnishings, which radiocarbon testing proved to be almost a thousand years old. This was proof that long before Columbus sailed to America other Europeans had landed and lived there, probably about the year 1000 B.C.

But for some reason the Norse left this Vineland, as they called it, never to return, and it wasn't until the early seventeenth century that Europeans came to what is now Canada to stay.

The early explorers were searching for a northern route to the spice islands of the East and Canada was just in the way. The first to come was an Italian named John Cabot. In 1497, he fought his way across the Atlantic Ocean in an English ship and landed on Cape Breton Island. He claimed the land for England, since he was sailing under the sponsorship of that country, and sailed back. A grateful king awarded him ten pounds, and that was that.

The next explorer was one of the most important ever to cross the Atlantic. His name was Jacques Cartier and he came from France.

In the summer of 1535, Cartier sailed his little ships up the Saint Lawrence River and was the first white man to see the great forests on the flat, fertile land along its banks. He was also the first Frenchman to endure the harsh Canadian winter. Where the city of Quebec now stands, he found an Indian village called Stadacona and there he decided to remain until the next spring. His ships were frozen in the ice, frigid gales tore at the flimsy garb of his sailors and, for lack of fresh food, many died of scurvy. Cartier returned to France, but he came back to the Saint Lawrence area once more. He failed to found a colony in the new world, however.

Almost fifty years later, Sir Humphrey Gilbert put ashore on the Newfoundland coast, where European fishermen had been landing to dry their catches for about a hundred years, and formally claimed the land for England.

Samuel de Champlain was the most important of all the French explorers. He sailed up the Saint Lawrence and the Ottawa rivers, and explored the land between Lakes Huron and Ontario. He founded Canada's first permanent colony at Quebec in 1608 and he began the fur trade with the Indians. But he made one terrible mistake. He helped the Huron and Algonquin Indians fight against the Iroquois, and, as a result, the most powerful Indians in the new world became his everlasting enemies.

The English laid further claim to Canada through the voyages of Henry Hudson, who perished somewhere on the icy waters of Hudson Bay, after his crew had mutinied and set him adrift.

The French wanted to do three things in the new land: begin a colony, reap the riches of the fur trade, and Christianize the Indians. The fur trade was the most successful of their objectives. Because of the abundance of beaver in Canadian waters and the popularity of beaver hats in Europe, this trade could make a daring man a fortune.

To get around the strict regulations and high license fees imposed by the French government, many bold young men took to the woods and lived as Indians. They were called *coureur de bois*—runners of the woods. Learning the woodcraft of the Indians, they pushed farther and farther up the unfrequented streams, seeking new trading territories.

The best known of these adventurers were Pierre Radisson and his brother-in-law, Chouart des Groseilliers. As a boy, Radisson was captured by the Indians, escaped, was recaptured and tortured, and finally was adopted by an Indian family. He escaped again and spent the rest of his days exploring and trading. He knew the Indian languages and the Indian ways, and he loved their rugged outdoor life.

Radisson and Groseilliers traveled overland as far as James Bay. Typical adventurers, they weren't particular about the people by whom they were employed. Angered over their mistreatment by French

*Indian guide and a young fisherman on a canoe trip through Canada's forest and lake country, where it is possible to live much as the old* coureurs de bois *lived two hundred years ago.*

authorities, they went to work for the English. For that country they explored Hudson Bay and other areas and set up trading posts.

The story of French Canada is filled with high adventure, great courage, and horrible violence.

The early settlers lived along the Saint Lawrence River in royal grants of land called siegniories. Each contained the home of the seignior, a church, a grist mill, and a stockade surrounded by a high pole fence. The habitant workers lived nearby and, in time of danger, sought protection within the fort.

On a beautiful autumn day in 1692, when the Saint Lawrence was like glass and the maple leaves were aflame, the Seigniory of Vercheres, twenty miles down river from the tiny settlement of Montreal, was in the charge of a fourteen-year-old girl, Madeleine de Vercheres. Her mother and father had both been called away on business and Madeleine had with her only her two brothers, aged ten and twelve, two soldiers, and an aged servant. It was thought the Iroquois would never attack this strong stockade.

But they did. Without warning, they came out of the bush, killed the workers, and attacked the fort. Madeleine took charge immediately. Issuing orders like a veteran soldier, she rallied her small band and, by cunning subterfuge, made the Indians think that the fort was defended by a full garrison. For eight days she fought on until help finally came.

There was constant strife between the white men, who were gradually taking over new land, and the Indians, who were determined to defend their rights. At Lachine, near the growing fur-trade center of Montreal, the Iroquois, under cover of a violent storm, surprised the village and killed two hundred men, women, and children. A hundred others were taken prisoner.

But gradually and inevitably the white men gained the upper hand and pushed farther and farther into new territory "for the glory of God and King."

Dollier and Galinee explored Lake Ontario, Lake Erie, and Lake Huron as far as Sault Ste. Marie. La Salle explored the Mississippi River to its mouth, following much the same route the priests Marquette and Jolliet had navigated earlier. La Verendrye and his sons voyaged west from Lake Superior through a chain of lakes and rivers to the south end of Lake Winnipeg, then farther west to the Black Hills area.

Meanwhile, the English were not idle. Long before La Verendrye went west, from Fort York on Hudson Bay, the young Hudson's Bay Company "servant," Henry Kelsey, journeyed south and west to the north end of Lake Winnipeg, and on into what is now northern Saskatchewan. He was perhaps the first white man to see the great herds of plains buffalo. Another Hudson's Bay Company man, Anthony Henday, traveled west as far as the spot where Red Deer, Alberta, now stands, and brought back some seventy loads of furs.

In the meantime, on the east coast, the French and English had been fighting for possession of Acadia, now Nova Scotia. The fort of Louisburg, now restored, on the tip of Cape Breton Island, changed hands many times, finally remaining in possession of the English. In 1749, the British built a naval base at Halifax.

The struggle between the French and English ended with the fall of Quebec to General Wolfe in 1759. On the renowned Plains of Abraham, now a historic monument, both the British general, Wolfe, and the French general, Montcalm, were killed. Wolfe, immortalized in song as "the dauntless hero," had his men scale the steep cliff on which the city of Quebec stood and surprise the French, who felt they were secure in their lofty fortress.

Under British rule, life in Canada was much the same as it had been under the French. Most French-Canadian settlers, having been guaranteed their rights of religion and language, and having no place to go, remained on their farms and in their villages. The fur trade continued to make men rich, but now the English merchants were in complete charge.

The American Revolution had a profound effect upon Canada. After independence was declared, about forty-five thousand persons who remained loyal to the British Crown sailed or trekked north to Canada, bringing their belongings with them. They settled on grants of land in New Brunswick, Nova Scotia, Prince Edward Island, around Montreal, along the upper Saint Lawrence River, and in the rich lands north of Lakes Ontario and Erie.

These United Empire Loyalists, as they were called, changed Canada from being mostly French-speaking to being mostly English-speaking. They settled on farms, built new towns, went into the lumber business, and set up a flourishing trade with Britain. They established Upper Canada (later Ontario), the dominant province of English Canada, and to a considerable extent they determined the social and political patterns of their new home.

And the west was opening up, too. Fur traders established posts along the Saskatchewan–Nelson River system as far west as the Rockies. Alexander Mackenzie, a determined Scotsman, reached the Pacific by going over the mountains. Later he and his hardy voyageurs paddled down the Mackenzie River to its mouth. Simon Fraser explored the raging Fraser River and David Thompson traversed and mapped much of the land east of the mountains and in them.

In 1792, Captain James Vancouver sailed into Burrard Inlet, near the mouth of the Fraser River, and surveyed much of the west coast north of there. Later settlements grew up on Vancouver Island and at the mouth of the Fraser. Timber, coal, and later gold brought thousands of pioneers to this land of abundance.

At the same time, settlers eager to plow the rich prairie soil and raise cattle were moving into the prairies by Red River carts, cargoe canoes, and river boats.

The fur trade still flourished and, in southern Alberta, unscrupulous traders, operating from the notorious "whisky forts" such as Fort

*Members of the famous Royal Canadian Mounted Police do much more than have their pictures taken by tourists. They travel thousands of miles by dog team or aircraft to supervise Eskimo villages. They police the widespread prairie towns and, all over Canada, they act as federal investigators.*

Whoopup, cheated the Indians of their furs in exchange for a cupful of cheap whisky.

In 1867, the most important event in Canadian history took place. Farsighted statesmen in Upper Canada (Ontario), Lower Canada (Quebec), and the Maritime Provinces worked to unite all the British colonies in North America into one country. By the British North American Act, a democratic federal system was established and Sir John A. Macdonald became the first prime minister of the country. Now economic, territorial, and political development had a federal as well as a provincial focus. Although only four provinces joined at the start, the way was open for the others when their time came. Canada was one country!

The new government soon faced a crisis. The Metis (mixed Indian and white blood people) who settled and hunted in the land around Lake Winnipeg became alarmed for their rights and titles and rebelled against the Crown. In 1874, after this Red River rebellion was put down, the government organized a federal police force to protect the Indians from unscrupulous whisky traders and the settlers against confused Indians, and to generally maintain law and order in the west.

This force was the famous Northwest Mounted Police (later renamed Royal Canadian Mounted Police). Their motto was—and is—*"Maintiens le Droit"* (Uphold the Right), and they earned a reputation for always getting their man. Whether or not this statement was completely true, the fact remains that, with the coming of the Mounties, outbreaks of crime became relatively rare in western Canada during late fur-trading and pioneer settlement times. And early forts such as Fort Walsh, Fort Calgary, Fort McLeod, and Fort Saskatchewan, from which the Mounties—often alone—set out on their long rides to investigate or prevent trouble among the white men and the Indians, were well known throughout the continent.

Shortly after this the railway was built across the plains, through the mountains, to the west coast, where "rail met keel." This was the unifying force of Canada, the real beginning of the country's development. Enticed by free homestead land, settlers poured in from eastern Canada, the United States, and Europe. Towns and cities grew up overnight. Land values boomed. The settlers staked their homesteads, built sod huts, gathered bleached buffalo bones for shipment east (they were used in manufacturing processes), plowed the prairie sod, and established their homes. Cities grew as distributing centers for the towns, and wheat became Canada's greatest export.

One by one, new provinces were formed from the territories, and took their place as self-governing units. The last of these, Newfoundland, oldest of all the British colonies, became Canada's tenth province in 1949. But it was not until 1964, three years before its one hundredth birthday, that Canada replaced the British red ensign, so proudly flown since 1759, with a new and distinctive Canadian flag, featuring a large maple leaf on a white background, with a broad band of red at each end.

*The Maple Leaf of Canada flies beside the Stars and Stripes of the United States at Niagara Falls, shared by the two friendly nations.*

# 4

# Rugged People of a Rugged Land

The people of Canada are as diverse and as rugged as the vast land they inhabit. They are North Temperate Zone people, which means that they must work hard to wrest a livelihood from reluctant nature. The land and water forms of this big country have greatly affected the lives and natures of its residents.

Take, for example, the Indians who inhabited Canada before the white men came. For each area there was a distinctive group. In the forests of the Canadian Shield and the Appalachians there were migratory woodland dwellers, hunters, and fishermen. They made the famous birchbark canoes, and their homes were dome-shaped wigwams built of sapling frames covered with bark.

In the Great Lakes area, where the soil and climate are suitable, the well-organized Indians were farmers as well as hunters. They cleared the land and grew corn, beans, and pumpkins, and they tapped the maple trees for the sweet sap. They resided in the famous long houses, skilfully constructed of poles and bark, grouped together in villages surrounded by a pole palisade.

On the prairies, where existence was hard, the Plains Indians followed wandering buffalo herds and subsisted almost entirely off them.

Mountain tribes survived by hunting deer, mountain sheep, and goats, and fishing in the deep lakes.

On the west coast, where conditions were easier, the Coast Indians made houses of flat boards split from the giant red cedar. For boats they hollowed out the same trees and, later, they carved them into colorful and intricate totem poles.

In the Arctic, Eskimos existed by hunting seal and bear, caribou and muskox.

In the southerly parts of the country, where the white men had use of the Indians' lands, they pushed back the red men onto reservations. Here the lives of the Indians completely changed. From being independent, they became dependent on government handouts. Some have left the reservations and work at trapping, commerce, farming, the professions or, as with the Mohawks of Caughnawaga, Quebec, on high steel construction.

In the north, where the white men had no use for the land but wanted valuable furs of the numerous animals found there, the Eskimos were converted from independent hunters to fur gatherers, dependent on the trading posts.

You will hear many conflicting stories about Eskimos. Some will say they dwell in snow houses and hunt. Others will maintain that this is nonsense—Eskimos live in tarpaper shacks and work for white men. Both are true. The Arctic is extremely wide—as wide as Canada—and what applies to one group of Eskimos does not necessarily apply to others.

Some groups of Eskimos, especially along the coast of the central Arctic, still live in igloos in winter, hunt with bone-tipped spears, and drive dog teams. In other places, such as Mary River on Baffin Island, Eskimos work in iron mines and drive bulldozers. Along the DEW (Distant Early Warning) Line, they work as tractor drivers, mechanics, and laborers. They reside in warm, prefabricated houses. Other Eskimos are trained as teachers, nurses, doctors, airline hostesses. Many of their children go to good local schools; others are picked up by aircraft, as children in other areas may be picked up by school buses. These children are taken to distant boarding schools for a term at a time, however. Then they are flown back to their homes.

The Mounties (the principal police force in the North), traders, missionaries, and teachers live well up there. Their houses are comfortably heated and furnished in a modern manner. Isolation is a thing of the past. The airplane can get them out of the Arctic in hours; the radio keeps them informed and entertained. They drive dog teams sometimes, but mostly gasoline-powered skidoos or the larger snowmobiles.

What of the white inhabitants of southern Canada? Despite modern transportation and communication, they, too, differ from each other from region to region. The Newfoundland fisherman speaks with a different accent from other Canadians. He says, "I come from Burgeo, me bye, and it's a some big place." The Newfoundlander lives close to nature as a miner, forest worker, or fisherman, and he has a great respect for nature's ways. It's true that the old fisherman's specialty of fish and bruise—made by boiling dried cod and mixing it with scrunchions (hard fried pork) and hardtack soaked in water—is now only eaten occasionally, but all Newfoundlanders are very much aware of their seagoing traditions.

At an early age, the boys—and girls, too—help their fathers with boats and they can handle a dory with skill and understanding.

The French Canadians, both in Quebec and in the other provinces, are quite different from other Canadians. For one thing, they speak French, and sing in French, and listen to French-language radio and television broadcasts. French is the language of the schoolroom. Most French Canadians are Roman Catholics, as, of course, are many other Canadians. As industry increases in Quebec, more and more young people leave their farms and villages of the river fronts and go to Montreal, Quebec, Three Rivers, Sherbrooke, or one of the other manufacturing centers.

And, most significant, the French Canadians are firmly determined to keep their culture and language. They feel that only by doing so can French Canadians make a worth-while contribution to their own race, to Canada, and to the world. Many English-speaking Canadians agree.

Ontario is the center of English Canada, the home of the WASPS—white, Anglo-Saxon Protestants. Since they live in the area most favored by nature, they are the richest Canadians. With their United Empire Loyalist background, they tend to be the most stanchly pro-British of all Canadians. There is a higher percentage of membership in the Church of England in Ontario than elsewhere.

Many boys and girls in Ontario go to private schools based on the English system, such as Upper Canada College (for boys), where cricket rather than baseball is the principal game.

But Ontario is changing, too. After World War II, hundreds of thousands of immigrants from non-British countries came to the province. They brought with them their own culture and language, and they are affecting the politics, entertainment, and laws of their adopted land.

For instance, before the war there were no Sunday sports or Sunday movies in Toronto. Now there are both.

West of the Great Lakes, the people of Canada are different again. In fact, it is almost as though they belonged to another country. Elsewhere in Canada, the prairie folk are known as "Westerners," and they have a reputation for being expansive, generous, and hospitable.

This reputation is undoubtedly owing to the isolation of pioneer days, when a traveler on a horse or driving a buggy simply stopped in at a lonely cabin at mealtime or bedtime and was given food and shelter.

The people of the prairies live in a big country and they think big. Also, they are of more diverse racial groups than Eastern Canadians. Besides the British and Americans, there are large colonies of Icelanders, Ukrainians, Poles, Mennonites, Germans, Swedes, and French Canadians.

Following the great discoveries of petroleum, natural gas, and potash in Alberta and Saskatchewan thousands of American businessmen and

*The harbor and lower town of Quebec City, capital of Quebec Province, as seen from the Citadel. The castle-shaped Hotel Frontenac is named for the Governor of New France who set out from here to subdue the Iroquois Indians in the seventeenth century.*

workers moved into the area. Calgary, Alberta, with almost thirty thousand American oilmen and their families, has been called "the most American city outside the United States."

For the most part, they are farmers or ranchers. On the immense flat farms of Saskatchewan, one man may work a thousand acres or more. He lives on the farm or in a nearby town. In many cases, he keeps no animals, except perhaps a dog and a cat, buys his milk from the dairy and his eggs from the grocer. In the spring, he puts in the wheat crop with high-powered machinery, and in the fall he takes it off with a combine. The rest of the time is pretty much his own for recreation and travel.

In politics he is likely to be a maverick. Saskatchewan farmers voted in the first socialist government in North America, which ruled the province for twenty years. Alberta and British Columbia have long had governments led by the Social Credit party, which has made little headway in Eastern Canada.

In Canada there is no western folklore such as exists in the United States, with its wild tales of cowboys and Indians, lynching of rustlers, strong, silent men, and shoot-outs on the main streets of boom towns. Rather there is a flamboyant tendency to tall stories, such as were found in the pioneer newspaper, *The Calgary Eyeopener.*

In the 1930's, when drought and grasshoppers devastated the plains, they told the story of the farmer who left a six-horse team in the field and returned to find that 'hoppers had eaten the animals and were pitching horseshoes for the harness.

To test the density of a dust storm, they said, you tossed a gopher into the air. If he dug a hole while aloft, it was real bad.

British Columbia, now, is a quite different part of Canada. Shut off from the rest of the country by the wall of the Rockies, and being so far distant from the federal capital, British Columbia has tended to go its own way. Even the early history of the province is not the same as that of the rest of Canada. Whereas development east of the Rockies came from the Saint Lawrence westward, most British Columbia settlers came in by ship. And, having access to the rest of the world through its own ports, great natural riches of forests, minerals, agricultural land, and water power, the province has been self-sufficient.

*Some 4-H members proudly display their Holstein calves for the judge at a country fair.*

Add to this the fact that British Columbia has the most clement climate in Canada and you have a people who are satisfied with their lot. "You couldn't pay me to live anywhere else," is a typical comment of a British Columbia resident.

So the people of Canada are not one people but at least six different groups of people—Arctic dwellers, Maritimers, French Canadians, Ontario residents, Westerners, and West Coasters. But they are all Canadians, united in their love of country and determination to have Canada play its part in shaping world events.

# 5

# Hello and Good-bye
# (Travel and Communications)

In a land 5,780 miles wide and comprising 3,851,809 square miles, getting from one place to another is a major problem. The difficulties of communication, too, are greater in Canada than in most other countries.

The first explorers and settlers traveled by boat and canoe. The famous voyageur canoe, thirty feet long by five feet wide, and weighing only 500 pounds, was a Canadian invention. It grew out of the necessity for a light, spacious, strong, cargo-carrying vessel that could navigate the turbulent river waters, but at the same time could be made and repaired right in the bush.

It had a light cedar frame, covered with strong sheets of birchbark sewn together with leather or root thongs, and made waterproof with pine gum on the seams. If one of these handy craft hit a rock and a hole was broken in the side, the voyageurs simply cut more bark and sewed it into place.

The voyageur canoe was manned by eight or ten gnome-like men, broad of shoulder, powerful of arms, and—preferably—short of legs. All day long they squatted in the canoe, paddling steadily and singing their paddling songs.

For more than a hundred years the voyageur canoe was the chief means of travel and transportation in Canada. Brigades of as many as fifty canoes set out from Montreal loaded with trade goods. The hazardous route took them up the Ottawa River to the Mattawa River, by means of which Lake Nipissing could be reached. After crossing the wide expanse of that lake, the brigade made its way by means of the French River into Georgian Bay. Then came a two-hundred-mile hazardous journey across the North Channel of Lake Huron, through the narrow passage of Sault Ste. Marie, and across Lake Superior. You can follow the voyageurs' route on the map.

At the west end of Superior, they went by way of the Pigeon River into the Rainy River-Lake of the Woods chain that took them, after many rough portages, to the south end of Lake Winnipeg. After paddling the full length of that lake (some two hundred and fifty miles), to the north end, they entered the Saskatchewan River system, which led them to the trading posts of the west.

Other routes led from ports on Hudson Bay into Lake Winnipeg.

Months or even years later, the brigade would return to Montreal with canoes loaded to the gunwales with furs given in exchange for their trade goods.

Not only traders, but trading company officials and their families, as well as settlers, traveled the same tortuous route by the same primitive means. In all kinds of weather they slept out on the ground under the upturned canoes. Small game, fish, pemmican, wild fruits, ship's biscuits, and pea soup so thick you could stand a paddle in it were their only fare.

Later, York boats and Durham boats and bateaux—all flat-bottomed vessels propelled by oars and sails—were used on the larger lakes and rivers.

On land, coaches, sleighs, and cutters were used, but the principal

*The York Boat, with its heavy keel, sails, and banks of oars, became the chief carrier of goods and people on Canadian waters in the early nineteenth century.*

freight carrier to the West was the famous Red River cart. This was a two-wheeled, high-axled contraption, pulled by one ox or pony. The wooden wheels on wooden axles set up such a screeching it could be heard for miles. Mosquitoes, dust storms, prairie fires, and sudden fierce thunderstorms plagued the métis drivers. Since the bushland of northern Ontario was impassable for land vehicles, the route to the West led through Chicago and St. Paul, and north to Fort Garry (now Winnipeg).

Red River carts were slow and bumpy and noisy, but they suited the rough prairie trails perfectly (when the brigade reached a river, the high wooden wheels were removed and tied beneath the carts to make a raft that could be floated across), and no one can estimate how many thousands of tons of desperately needed freight were carried to the West on their creaking frames.

But canoe and river boat and cart all disappeared abruptly when the railway was built across Canada, reaching the west coast in the autumn of 1885. The tremendous task of laying railway tracks across the rocky terrain of the Canadian Shield, over the flat miles of prairie, and through the mountains to the coast is one of the engineering wonders of the century. And to a large extent the railway made Canada. Because of it, thousands of settlers and their effects could be transported to the fertile plains. The millions of bushels of grain they produced could be carried to Lake Superior, and thence through the Great Lakes and the Saint Lawrence to the Atlantic. Lumber could be carried from west coast sawmills to build the prairie settlers' homes; fish and fruits for their tables came from the same area. Plows, binders, stoves, clothing, and hundreds of other manufactured goods could be shipped from the factories of Ontario and Quebec to fill the settlers' needs. Without the railway, the development of Canada would have been painfully slow.

Closely following the railway came the telegraph—man's first means of rapid communication. The "talking wires," as the amazed Plains Indians called them, carried news almost instantaneously. Now the people of Vancouver knew what was taking place in Ottawa within minutes of its happening. Grain prices, shipping schedules, and other vital information could be sent across the country within a short time.

Also, at about the same time, a Canadian, Alexander Graham Bell,

*Toronto's International Airport has parking on the roof, reached by a ramp.*

invented the telephone. Soon new humming lines followed the railway tracks, and a housewife in Vancouver could talk to her friend in Halifax. Canada was truly united.

Other advances in travel and communication followed rapidly. A Canadian carriage maker, Robert McLaughlin, built the first McLaughlin automobile in 1907, and for years this rugged car bumped over the roads of the country. Later, it became the mainstay of the great General Motors complex.

But it has been air travel that has made the greatest difference in this immense land. In 1909, John McCurdy flew the *Silver Dart*, designed by Alexander Graham Bell, over the frozen lake at Baddeck, Nova Scotia. This was the first flight in the British Empire. During the 1914–1918 war, Canadian pilots were among the most successful of all the Allied fliers. After the war, many of the same Canadian pilots became the famous "bush pilots" who flew men and cargo into the immensely rich territories of the Canadian Shield and the North. Following the 1939–1945 war, air travel and transportation developed rapidly. Today it is possible for a businessman to finish a good day's work in Toronto, board a trans-Canada plane, and be in Vancouver in time for a dinner meeting on the same day.

Radio networks across Canada virtually ended isolation for thousands of farmers, bush workers, fishermen, miners, and ranchers, who, by necessity, live far from centers of population. Television, an extension of radio, has completed the process of instant communication. A microwave system was built across the country, carrying live programs from coast to coast. Today, Canadians use radio and television as extensively as any people anywhere.

# 6

## God Save the Queen

Perhaps nothing about Canada is more baffling to outsiders than her form of government. As a matter of fact, it is baffling to many Canadians. The national anthem is "God Save the Queen," but many public functions are opened with the singing of both "The Queen" and another anthem, "O Canada." Often, notably in Quebec, but elsewhere, too, "O Canada" is the only song used.

The Governor General, who is the representative of the British Crown in Canada, must sign all legislation before it becomes law. But he is a Canadian, selected by the Canadian parliament. Almost without exception, he acts entirely on the advice of that parliament.

Canada is a democracy. The people have, if they care to exercise it, complete control of their own affairs. But the constitution, as it stands, cannot be amended except by an act of the British parliament.

A quick look at Canada's political development since 1759 will help us to understand the present condition. The first act passed by the British parliament (Quebec Act 1774) provided that the colony of Canada should be ruled by a governor appointed by the Crown, and an executive council, also appointed. No elected representatives of the people had any say in the government.

Then came the American Revolution, and it affected Canadian political affairs in two ways. First, the British parliament changed its attitude toward "colonies." Second, the thousands of United Empire Loyalists who came to Canada were accustomed to and demanded some measure of self-government.

Thus, the Constitutional Act of 1791 provided for an elected legislative assembly as part of the government of Canada. Unfortunately, however, all effective power was in the hands of an appointed executive council, and the assembly had no real power. Elections were held and good men sent to the assemblies of both Upper and Lower Canada. They could debate and argue and propose, but they could not enact legislation. In one session of the assembly alone fifty-eight reform measures were passed, but all were turned down by the powers above them.

But good men are never content to accept injustice lying down. And there were other injustices. Clergy Reserves, for instance, provided that one-seventh of Crown land be set aside for the Protestant clergy—which was interpreted to mean only the Church of England, although Methodists and Presbyterians were plentiful in the colonies. The lack of municipal institutions was another serious weakness, along with the tendency for political power to be concentrated in the hands of an "in" group—the Family Compact in Upper Canada and the Château Clique in Lower Canada.

So there was rebellion. Led by the fiery Scotsman, William Lyon Mackenzie in Upper Canada, and Louis Joseph Papineau in Lower Canada, the "radicals" took up arms against the King. But it was a fizzle. In Upper Canada there was one short, ignoble engagement where, after one volley from the militia, the disorganized, poorly armed rebels broke and ran. In Lower Canada there was more fighting but the result was the same. The rebellion was crushed, and the leaders were hanged or exiled.

But, although the rebellion failed miserably, much good came of it. Lord Durham was sent to Canada by the British government to investigate grievances, and he wrote a report in which he advocated responsible government for Canada. The Act of Union in 1840 united Upper and Lower Canada and laid the groundwork for responsible government by the people's elected representatives.

The first parliament under the new act was called together in Kingston in 1841. In 1849, the Governor General, Lord Elgin, signed a bill passed by the assembly, although he personally disagreed with it. Responsible government was a fact. From now on, the majority would rule.

Thus political freedom was won in Canada. The British North America Act of 1867 established a federal system with certain well-defined powers allotted to the provincial and federal governments. It remains the same today.

*The House of Commons in session. The Speaker of the House, seated at one end, enforces the rules.*

If any day were to be proclaimed as a Canadian "Independence Day," it would be December 11, 1931. For on that day, by the Statute of Westminster, all the minor restrictions to Canada's sovereignty were abolished, and she assumed complete control of her domestic and foreign affairs.

The party system obtains in Canada. There must be an election at least every five years. The leader of the political party electing the majority of members to the House of Commons (out of a total of 265) becomes the Prime Minister. The Prime Minister must be an elected member of the House of Commons, and he is completely responsible to it. If he and his cabinet members (also members of the Commons) propose a piece of legislation to Parliament and it is defeated, he must resign as Prime Minister. The leader of the opposition—if he has sufficient support in the Commons to do so—may become Prime Minister. Otherwise, a general election will be called so that the voters can decide the issue.

Since the Canadian system of government is often compared with that of the United States, it is interesting to note some of the essential differences:

— The Prime Minister must, in all things, have the support of the majority of members in the House of Commons;

— The Senate, made up of one hundred and two members, is often re-

40

ferred to as the Upper House. But its members are appointed for life by the government, usually from the party in power, and the Senate has little lawmaking power.

— There is rarely any party politics in municipal elections. Mayors, reeves, councilmen, school board members, run as independents, and are elected as such;

— Officials of the courts—judges, Crown prosecutors, sheriffs, etc., are appointed and not elected. Unless they commit a crime or resign voluntarily, they keep their positions for life;

— No one votes directly for the Prime Minister as such, except the voters in the constituency where he happens to be running for election. Each voter votes for his own local candidate only. The leader with a majority of supporters elected becomes Prime Minister.

There are numerous other differences, but these are the most important ones.

The government of each province is essentially the same as the federal government, except that the leader is called the Premier, and in all provinces except Quebec there is no Upper House.

*Her Majesty Elizabeth II opens a session of the Canadian Parliament.*

# 7

# A Land of Great Cities

Although Canada is often thought of as a land of farms, ranches, forests, and lakes—which it is—it is also a land of huge modern cities. These fall roughly into three categories: port cities, manufacturing centers, and distributing centers. The two largest cities, Montreal and Toronto, are a combination of all three.

Montreal is at once Canada's largest and most glamorous city. Founded by the Frenchman, Sieur de Maisonneuve, in 1642 as a religious refuge in the bush (originally it was named City of Mary—Ville Marie), its natural advantages soon led to great commercial development.

Montreal is situated on an island in the Saint Lawrence at the mouth of the Ottawa River and, because of the rapids, this was as far up the Saint Lawrence as ocean ships could go. So Montreal became the principal port of Canada and the center of the fur trade. In turn, it became Canada's principal lumber shipping port, wheat shipping port, and leading manufacturing center. Its natural surroundings favored Montreal in other ways. The land around is fertile and flat; the Canadian Shield to the north provides quantities of minerals and almost limitless forests; the abrupt fall of the Saint Lawrence at this point, and of the rivers roaring down from the Shield, provides abundant water power. Never was a city so fortunate.

Because of its large French-speaking population, Montreal's culture is varied and lively. It is the hub of French-language broadcasting, drama, folk festivals, and education, and the University of Montreal is the home of much modern French-Canadian thought.

Toronto, situated on the north shore of Lake Ontario, near the western end of the lake, is Canada's second largest city. But, strangely

*The old and the new in Montreal, Quebec. Sidewalk sippers relax near St. James Cathedral, with the ultra-modern Place Ville Marie office building towering above.*

enough, it was founded one hundred and fifty years later than was Montreal, and it was chosen rather for its military advantage than for anything else. In 1793, John Graves Simcoe, first Lieutenant Governor of Upper Canada, decided that the colony's capital at Newark (now Niagara-on-the-Lake) was too vulnerable to American attack, and so he sailed across the lake, selected a good harbor where a fur-trading post had once stood, built Fort York and made it his capital.

Being a military garrison and capital combined, the town naturally prospered, but, as well, it was situated on excellent land in the heart of fertile southern Ontario. Electricity from the great falls at Niagara provided power for its factories.

Being so favored, Toronto grew as naturally as a healthy boy who gets plenty of nourishment. The abundance of power, the agricultural products, and minerals and forests of the Canadian Shield soon made Toronto English Canada's leading manufacturing and financial city. It is also the educational and cultural center of English Canada. The headquarters of the English network of the Canadian Broadcasting Corporation are there, as are most of the magazine and book publishers. The University of Toronto is the largest in Canada.

*Toronto, capital of Ontario, as seen at night from the harbor.*

Toronto was the first Canadian city to build a subway. It is also the home of the Canadian National Exhibition, described as the largest permanent exhibition in the world, which attracts millions of excited visitors every summer.

Vancouver, British Columbia, has been called "the smuggest city in Canada." This, of course, is unjust. But the fact remains that anybody who lives there will tell you without hesitation that Vancouver is the most beautiful, the most progressive, the best-planned city in Canada—and has the finest climate. Where else, they will ask, have you got mountains right in the city? Where else can you go swimming in the Pacific and fishing for salmon and yachting—right in the city? And where will you find a park like Stanley Park, with its giant red cedar trees big enough to drive a car through, its totem poles, and the finest zoo in the country? Where can you see ships from Japan, Australia, Los Angeles, Honolulu, Hong Kong, coming and going under beautiful Lion's Gate Bridge?

And it's mostly true. Vancouver is Canada's biggest west coast port. From it is shipped wheat to China, lumber to the United States, and many other countries, fruit and fish to the markets of the world, potash from the mines of Saskatchewan, coal from Alberta.

It is Canada's third largest city and is growing rapidly. High-rise apartments, thirty and more stories high, spring up like mushrooms around the downtown section. A farseeing and energetic urban-renewal program is replacing old buildings with modern ones. As the city becomes more and more industrialized, new attractive factories appear in designated areas.

From Horseshoe Bay in West Vancouver large ferries carry people and automobiles across the strait to Victoria on the tip of Vancouver Island. And the latter beautiful city, where flowers bloom all year round, has an even better climate than Vancouver. It is the capital of British Columbia, and a favorite spot for British ex-patriots who find there a bit of "olde England."

Edmonton, Alberta, is one of Canada's most remarkable cities. In the first place, it is the farthest north of any sizable city in North America. In the beginning, its growth was gradual and steady. Situated on the north branch of the Saskatchewan River, it was an important fur-trading fort. Great deposits of coal lie beneath the city itself, and the surrounding farm land is rich and comparatively well watered. Edmonton district farmers boast that they've never had a crop failure.

But two recent developments have made Edmonton into the "Boom city of the North." One is the development of the Canadian Arctic. Every day huge cargo planes leave Edmonton airport, carrying engineers, supplies, building materials, and heavy equipment northward to some new mineral development. From Edmonton, there is a direct air route over the Arctic to Europe. It is also connected with the busy Alaska Highway.

Calgary, in southern Alberta, is best known for the flamboyant Calgary Stampede, held there every July, for Calgary is a cattle city. But it is also an oil and gas city. The surrounding fields attract oil men from the United States and Europe. It is a lively city—a city of big talk and big deeds, expansive as the rolling land that surrounds it.

The other important prairie cities are Winnipeg, the capital of Manitoba; Regina, the capital of Saskatchewan; and Saskatoon, Sas-

*For action, speed, thrills, and chills, you can't beat the chuckwagon race at the Calgary Stampede.*

katchewan, a distributing center for the central portion of the province.

Winnipeg has been called the "grain center" of Canada. Through it pass the long, long trains carrying the prairie crop to the ports of Eastern Canada. It has also been called "the gateway to the West" because the main lines of both the Canadian National and the Canadian Pacific railways run through the city. Winnipeg has the largest railway yards in Canada.

Winnipeg also has the doubtful distinction of being the only city in the country to be regularly hit by floods. The Red River, flowing over the flat lands to the south, is normally slow-running and peaceful. But melting snow and heavy spring rains can make it a raging torrent that carries away farms and inundates suburban homes.

Regina—originally named Pile of Bones—because of the quantities of bleached buffalo bones found there by the first settlers—is the flattest city in Canada. It sits on the Regina Plain—once a glacial lake—like a dish on a flat table. You can see for miles in every direction. Long a distribution point for the prairie towns that surround it, Regina has also benefited from riches that lie deep beneath the soil—oil, natural gas, and potash.

Ottawa, Ontario, Canada's capital, is located on the bank of the Ottawa River, where the Rideau flows in from the south and the Gatineau from the north. On the south side of the river is the rich, flat farm land of the Ottawa Valley; on the north side, the beautiful, tree-covered Gatineau Hills, noted for their ski resorts.

The city is now and always has been a center of the forest industry. Pulp mills, sawmills, and a large match plant are found in and around the city.

But, as in any national capital, Ottawa's biggest industry is the government. In 1857, to settle a dispute between Montreal, Toronto, and a number of other cities as to which would be the capital, Queen Victoria was requested to choose between them. She wisely chose the little town, Ottawa, which wasn't even in the running. Since then, of course, the city has prospered until now it is Canada's sixth largest city. The site of the parliament buildings, looking over the river, is beautiful and impressive.

Hamilton, Ontario, is the leading steel-manufacturing city of Canada, and the supplier to the other manufacturing cities that form "the golden horseshoe" around the southwest end of Lake Ontario. Hamilton has an excellent port for bringing in iron ore from the Lake Superior and Labrador iron-producing districts, and for shipping out manufactured goods both ways through the Saint Lawrence Seaway. McMaster University is an important focal point for studies of water pollution in the Great Lakes.

Southern Ontario, being the most densely populated area of Canada,

*The beautiful legislative buildings at Winnipeg, capital of Manitoba.*

has, of course, the most cities. Windsor, across the river from Detroit, was for a long time the leading automobile manufacturing area in Canada, but now it is rivaled by Oshawa and Oakville. London, Ontario, is a large, gracious city, named after London, England, and situated on the Thames River which runs into Lake Saint Clair.

The oldest and most picturesque Canadian city is, of course, Quebec. There the visitor can walk along the top of the original stone wall that protected the city from attack three hundred years ago, and can look down from the citadel on Cape Diamond at the ships in the Saint Lawrence, as the beleaguered garrison looked down on the ships of General Wolfe.

And he can walk on the green, green grass of the Plains of Abraham and down the steep ravine of Wolfe's Cove and ponder how foot soldiers ever hauled the cannons up there.

The first hospital in Canada, the Hotel Dieu, still stands close to the old wall, and still administers to the sick. The Ursuline Convent is still there, too, and within its walls the Catholic sisters still draw water from the oldest well in Canada.

But the narrow, crooked, history-filled streets of the old town are only part of Quebec. The city is now an important shipping and manufacturing center. Huge rafts of pulpwood, cut in the Laurentian Hills, are floated down the river to mills in the town. The manufacture of fur goods, clothing, and tobacco products is also important.

Each year, the Quebec Winter Carnival attracts thousands of young and old to the historic city. For days there is fun for all—tobogganing on the long run in front of the Château Frontenac, a popular old hotel, boat races through the ice chunks on the river, pageants, and merriment in the streets.

The three Atlantic port cities—Saint John's, Newfoundland; Saint John, New Brunswick, and Halifax, Nova Scotia—are also rich in history. On Signal Hill, in Saint John's, you can stand and look out over old cannons that once guarded the port from French attack. Or in the crescent-shaped harbor you can watch fishing boats and fishermen from Portugal or France fitting out for the next cod-fishing trip to the Grand Banks. Or you can stroll along the water front, remembering that here, before Columbus ventured across the Atlantic, Basque fishermen landed to take on water and dry their fish.

At Halifax, you can see the great inner and outer basins where, during the two world wars, dozens of fighting ships lay at anchor, taking on supplies for the bitter battle of the North Atlantic.

It was in this same harbor that the largest and most devastating explosion Canada has known occurred. On December 6, 1917, a French ammunition carrier, loaded with hundreds of tons of high explosives, hit a Norwegian freighter, caught fire, and blew up. Every building in Halifax was damaged. Schools collapsed like cardboard buildings, a tidal wave wrecked the water front. A half-ton ship's anchor was found two miles away. All told, sixteen hundred people were killed, and thousands more were injured.

At Saint John, New Brunswick, where the highest tides in the world roar in and out of the Bay of Fundy, you can see how they spill into the Saint John River with such force as to make the river run backward over the famous Reversing Falls, and watch the cargo ships from the West Indies unloading their bananas, pineapples, and other fruits, along with tons of sugar cane to be refined in Saint John. And there, too, you can see ships being refitted in one of the largest dry docks in the world.

Names of other cities and towns in Canada often make visitors shake their heads in wonder. In addition to London, Ontario, on the River Thames, there is Stratford on the Avon. There's Medicine Hat in Alberta and Moose Jaw in Saskatchewan. (Some say a medicine man lost his hat at one place and a settler mended a cart with a moose's jaw at the other.) Newfoundland is richest in odd place names, such as Cow Head and Bay Bulls, Witless Bay and Empty Basket Cove, and Bay D'Espoir (hope), which everybody calls Bay Despair.

# 8

# What Do You Do in Your Spare Time?

Canadians love sports, and spend more time playing, watching, and talking about games than they do on politics. Stop anyone on the street in any season and you can get an argument about the merits of the Toronto Maple Leaf or Montreal Canadiens hockey teams . . . or the Winnipeg Blue Bombers and Edmonton Eskimos football teams . . . or who will win the famous Macdonald Briar curling bonspiel.

And the Canadians use and enjoy their big land with its surprising contrasts. During the summer holidays, the highways and bush roads are full of campers, hikers, and sight-seers. Fishing, duck hunting, deer hunting, and big-game hunting are enjoyed by thousands. The hundreds of provincial and national parks are crowded every summer. Winter carnivals, too, attract dog-sled drivers, skidoo racers, and enthusiastic spectators from far afield.

Lacrosse is Canada's oldest game and, until hockey took over, it was the national sport. When the first French settlers arrived in North America, they found Indians playing something they called baggataway. Each player carried a stick about three feet long, with a curved end encircling a loose deer-hide webbing. With this they tossed a hard ball back and forth and tried to put it in goals at the ends of the field. It was a fast-running, rough contest, with players often getting banged on the head.

The white men took to the game and, as they did with everything else they found, began changing it to suit themselves. They drew up a list of rules providing for twelve men to a team, and a field 125 yards long and 110 yards wide. Eventually, baggataway evolved into lacrosse. In 1925, a Canadian Lacrosse Association was formed, and a solid-gold cup was put up for competition.

Today lacrosse is popular in two main areas—Southern British Co-

*Hockey players, like the baseball players of the United States and the skiers of Sweden, are heroes in Canada. Many of the players on American professional teams have come from Canada.*

lumbia and Southern Ontario. The Indians from Brantford, Ontario, are still among the best players. The game is played on a surface the size of a hockey rink, usually indoors, with six players on a team. Each year, national championships are played off between Ontario and British Columbia teams, and attract a relatively small but highly enthusiastic coterie of spectators.

But ice hockey is really Canada's leading sport today. Canadians invented it, and Canadian professional hockey players are the best in the world. Practically every Canadian boy plays hockey. As soon as the first ice begins to form in November, out come the skates, hockey sticks, shin guards, and pucks. Prairie farm kids play it on the frozen sloughs. Ontario and Quebec kids play it on the frozen rivers and lakes. Suburban fathers spend many frigid hours making backyard rinks. Every village, no matter how small, has at least one outdoor rink, and arenas with artificial ice are a "must" in larger communities.

In many areas "little leagues" are organized by service clubs and others, and teams travel by bus from town to town. From these leagues the best players graduate into teams of the Canadian Amateur Hockey Association. Here they play juvenile, junior, and senior hockey and, at the end of each season, there are championship play-offs between teams of Western Canada and Eastern Canada for the Memorial Cup (Junior) and the Allan Cup (Senior).

It is the ambition of every good hockey player to become a professional and gain fame and fortune in the National Hockey League. Players such as the fabulous Gordie Howe, Rocket Richard, and Bobby Hull are national heroes. All the good amateur players are closely watched by scouts from the professional teams. They are signed to a contract as soon as possible, and from that time on are the property of the parent team. They toil on various "farm teams" in Buffalo, New

York, or Tulsa, Oklahoma, or Vancouver, in Canada, until they are ready for the big time.

The culmination of the hockey season is, of course, the Stanley Cup play-offs. Canadian fans are just as likely to be rooting for Chicago, Detroit, or one of the other American teams as they are for Toronto or Montreal. Nearly all the players are Canadian anyway, and when Gordie Howe scores a goal in the Detroit arena, the people of the tiny community of Floral, Saskatchewan, where he was born—watching it on television—know the greatest joy of all.

And that brings us to curling. In Canada, curling isn't so much a game as a way of life. In small towns throughout the land the curling rink has long been the focal point of social activities during the long, cold, dreary winter months. The prairie pioneer, miles away from his neighbor and thousands of miles from the entertainment centers, used to pile into the cutter of an evening and head for the curling rink in town. Here, in the warmth of the waiting rooms, he would meet his friends and—when he wasn't on the ice playing—watch and comment loudly on how well other players were doing. Farmers do the same thing today, except that they travel in automobiles and curl on artificial ice.

A good deal of curling's popularity comes from the fact that it can be played equally well by young and old, male and female. You need a sheet of smooth, level ice at least 50 yards long and 10 feet wide, eight players—four on each rink—each equipped with two 40-pound curling rocks. The idea is simple. You take turns sliding the rocks from one end of the rink to the other, and see which rink can get the most rocks closest to the button. It's permitted to knock the other team's rocks out of the way with yours and to help the progress of your teammates' rocks by sweeping vigorously in front of them with a long-strawed broom.

The game is good exercise, it's played healthily in the fresh air, and it's sociable. Every Canadian community is equipped with at least one curling rink, containing numerous sheets of ice. It's a shouting, kidding, fun-type game, and most vigorous Canadians over the age of sixteen spend a great deal of time at it. There are numerous competitions—called bonspiels—culminating in the Macdonald Briar, when the best rinks from ten provinces play off. The winner then represents Canada in the international Scotch Cup bonspiel, which Canada nearly always wins.

Football is played in Canada much as it is in the United States, except that the field is a little longer and wider, there are twelve men instead of eleven on a team, and the attacking team has three downs instead of four in which to gain ten yards or give up the ball. Also, there are a few minor scoring differences. Just as Canada supplies American professional hockey teams with players, the colleges of the United States provide much of the manpower for the ten Canadian professional football teams. Four of these teams make up the Eastern Conference (Hamilton, Ottawa, Montreal, Toronto), and five the Western Conference (Vancouver, Edmonton, Calgary, Regina, Winnipeg). Another Toronto team is in the Continental League. In early December of each year, the winning teams of the two conferences play off for the Grey Cup, seen on television from coast to coast—and the country goes football crazy!

Canadians enjoy many other sports, most of them winter sports. At one time snowshoeing was popular. In Montreal and Toronto large snowshoe clubs were formed and extensive hikes organized. But snowshoeing has given way to skiing, which is getting more and more popular each year. North of Montreal, in the fabulous Laurentian Hills, there are many ski resorts with modern lifts and good accommodations. Ontario and the Maritime Provinces are also well supplied with good ski hills and resorts. But it is in the Rockies of British Columbia and Alberta that the best skiing is to be had. Jasper and Banff are famous for their mountain ski runs, and the citizens of Vancouver can

*Skating and curling are favorite sports in Canada, for young and old, feminine and masculine players.*

ski within the city limits. Bobsledding and tobogganing are popular with children all over Canada.

The principal spring games in Canada have always been baseball and softball. In Saskatchewan, particularly, the annual Sports Day (often on the 24th of May, a national holiday in honor of the birthday of Queen Victoria) is primarily a baseball tournament. Teams from a number of towns, often bolstered by professional players from south of the international border, compete for prize money. It's a great day, often sunny, sometimes hot, and always windy. The spectators ring the ball diamond with their new cars and honk their horns in appreciation of good plays. The women's softball tournament is going on at the same time, and children are having their own games.

Professional baseball has never really been so successful in Canada as either professional hockey or football. Some of the larger cities have teams in the international leagues, but mostly the fans are content to watch American and National League baseball games on television.

Canada has been called the "vacation land of North America," and certainly there is the space, the wild game, the scenery, the variety of terrain, and the public and private resorts for millions of people to enjoy themselves.

The fishing has always been fabulous, but, until recently, to a large extent inaccessible. Now air travel has changed that. A harried executive in Montreal or New York can hop into a small, pontoon-equipped plane and, within an hour or so, land in a remote northern lake full of fish. After catching his quota, he can pack them aboard and have them for a late dinner at home, if he so wishes. The same trip would have taken Pierre Radisson months to complete.

Canada's national parks are known throughout the North American continent—and abroad, too. There are thirty of these parks altogether but we will describe only a few of the best-known ones here.

Most famous of all the parks are those in the Canadian Rockies—Banff, Jasper, Waterton Lakes, Mount Revelstoke, Glacier, Yoho, and Kootenay. Jasper, the largest and farthest north of these, has an area of 4,200 square miles and some of the most breathtakingly beautiful mountain peaks on the continent. It is a naturalist's paradise. Fuzzy mountain sheep graze on the lower slopes, and the famous mountain goats leap precariously among the higher crags. Your car will often have to slow down on the highway to avoid missing a lumbering mother black bear and her two cubs, one of which may be brown. Elk, deer, and moose feed quietly in mountain meadows. Towering, snow-capped peaks surround you on all sides. And you can visit the famous Columbia icefields, source of water for the mighty Saskatchewan River.

Banff National Park, southeast of Jasper, is famous throughout the world for its summer and winter attractions. It has been called "twenty-five hundred square miles of beauty," and it lives up to its name. Lake Louise, for instance, has appeared on so many post cards, sent to so many countries, that one might expect, on actually seeing it, to be unimpressed. But when you do catch sight of it, bluer than any lake could possibly be, with the mist-shrouded mountain forming a perfect backdrop against the whiteness of the glacier—it takes the breath away.

And you can have as much fun whether you stay at the fabulous Banff Springs Hotel at $100 a day or bunk down in your own tent in the well-equipped campgrounds. You view the same mountains, ride the same ponies along the same trails, and enjoy the same hot water that pours from the famous hot springs.

East of the Rockies, located on Alberta's northern boundary, is the largest park in Canada, 17,300 square miles of bush, prairie, marsh, rivers, and lakes. It was here, in Wood Buffalo National Park, that famous naturalists from the United States and Canada searched for and found the nesting grounds of the elusive and almost extinct whooping cranes. It is also the home of a tremendous herd of wood buffalo, an adaptation of the buffalo of the plains.

Saskatchewan's biggest park is north of Prince Albert. It is a favorite spot for canoeists who want to rough it in the wilderness by traveling for hundreds of miles through its chain of lakes and rivers. And the fishing is great all the way.

Riding Mountain National Park in Manitoba is a camper's paradise— 1,148 square miles of forest and clear, clear lakes. Here you can really get away from the roar of city traffic and, if you are willing to rough it, you may even get away from the roar of outboard motors. There's plenty of room for everyone and you're sure to see deer, moose, elk, bear, beaver, and wild buffalo.

The biggest park in Ontario, Algonquin Park, is not a national park but a provincial park. Here 1,754,240 acres of forests, rivers, and lakes are within easy driving distance of heavily settled southern Ontario. Canoe trips in the park are a tradition, and at night you can hear the howl of the timber wolf.

But don't be afraid. Despite their reputation for eating people, there is no proven record of anybody in Canada ever having been even bitten by a healthy wolf. The Ontario Department of Lands and Forests catches wolves in the park and straps tiny radio transmitters to their necks so that their every movement can be followed. They've got a few wolves in pens, too, for the tourists to pat, and if you howl at them in the right key, they'll obligingly howl right back at you.

Deer stand by the side of the road, looking noble and trying to induce tourists to stop and give them popcorn, candy, or other goodies. This must never be done under any circumstances, however. One important reason is that these are wild animals and they may lose the ability to forage for themselves in their normal way, or they may not build up sufficient physical resistance to survive the winter because of improper diet. As a result, they may die of starvation when the tourists have gone home.

Residents of the province of Quebec and visitors are particularly well served with parks. La Verendrye Park, 140 miles northwest of Montreal, is almost twice as big as Algonquin Park, and it is full of lakes and rivers and fish. The government maintains twelve fishing camps for visitors.

But the most famous Quebec park is Mont Tremblant. With a mountain 3,150 feet high, more than forty miles of ski trails, and quaint habitant-style cottages for the guests, it attracts hundreds of thousands of skiers every year.

Every province, in fact, has dozens of national and provincial parks, and every year more visitors enjoy them. In Nova Scotia, Cape Breton National Park is all but encircled by the famous Cabot Trail that winds along the cliffs overlooking the rocky Atlantic shore. Fundy National Park in New Brunswick is great for ocean bathing and deep sea fishing.

Prince Edward Island National Park boasts twenty-five miles of fine ocean beach and the home of *Anne of Green Gables.* In rugged Newfoundland, Terra Nova National Park looks out over the Atlantic.

There are, of course, many National Historic Sites, too. One of the most popular of these—with Canadians—is Brock's Monument at Queenston Heights where, on October 13, 1812, the British forces defeated the Americans with heavy losses to the invaders. Another is Crysler's Farm, on the Saint Lawrence River, where about a year later a British force of 600 men stopped an American army of 7,000 on its way to attack Montreal. At least these are the Canadian versions of the events.

Public education is as good in Canada as in any country in the world. Every child, no matter whether he lives in a big city or in the Yukon, has the opportunity to obtain free education, both elementary and secondary.

In the provinces, schools are built and operated by local elected school boards, and financed by municipal taxation and grants from the provincial governments. In the territories, education is the responsibility of the Department of Northern Affairs.

The old one-room schoolhouses that since pioneer days dotted the rural areas of Canada have all but disappeared. And a good thing. They were a stopgap at best, poorly lighted, cold in winter, hot in summer, and terribly poorly equipped. (The Saskatchewan school where this writer struggled, as a youth, to teach the children of the area for $450 a year in 1933 is now being used as a wheat granary.)

In place of the one-room shacks run by local school boards, the rural districts have consolidated and built large, modern schools—properly lighted, well heated, and equipped with modern aids to teaching and learning. The teachers are well paid and highly skilled.

Radio and television, along with movies, are used extensively in Canadian schools. Through the Canadian Broadcasting Corporation's School Broadcast System, and those sponsored by provincial departments of education, classes tune in to the best in drama, poetry, actuality broadcasts, scientific demonstrations, and so on.

Each of the provinces has its own university and, in the more populous provinces, there may be three or more. There is considerable exchanging with professors from other countries. Thus Sir William Osler, a graduate of McGill University in Montreal who won international renown as a physician and teacher, lectured at McGill, Johns Hopkins, and Oxford.

Other Canadian graduates who have become world famous include Sir Frederick Banting and Charles Best of the University of Toronto who discovered insulin and thus saved millions of lives; Dr. Harold Johns of the University of Saskatchewan who developed the first cobalt bomb for the treatment of cancer, and Dr. Wilder Penfield, a McGill neurosurgeon who broke new ground in his explorations of the human brain.

Worth-while Canadian writers? There have been far too many to cover in the short space available. For this reason, having been born and having lived all my life in Canada, I shall mention only those Canadian writers who, for one reason or another, have impressed me.

Robert Service was my first favorite. Not because he is the best Canadian poet, far from it, but because his poems about the hard, cold life of the Yukon gold rush struck a responsive chord in a Saskatchewan boy. When Canadians read about "the cussedest land that I know" and "where the mighty mountains bare their fangs unto the moon," they know exactly what Service is talking about. Many a schoolboy has memorized his poems just for the fun of it, and I'm sure that says something for a poet.

Then there was Ernest Thompson Seton, who wrote the best boys-and-nature books ever. A whole generation of Canadians became Yan of *Two Little Savages* whenever they crawled into a tent or smelled the moldy moss of the deep woods. This is still true with young people all over the world.

Another favorite was Charles G. D. Roberts, a fine writer of nature stories. Perhaps he wasn't always scientifically accurate, but few boys or girls care too much for that. What they do care for and never forget is the warm understanding they gain of the hard fight for survival of all birds and animals.

The first Canadian novelist I remember and one who made a lasting impression was Ralph Connor, the Winnipeg preacher whose real name was Charles Gordon. He wrote about the tall, powerful, God-fearing

58

Scotsmen who cut timber along the Ottawa Valley and floated log rafts down the river. And he could stir the blood.

When I was a boy delivering papers in Saskatoon, Saskatchewan, I used to chuckle over a syndicated column by a McGill University professor, Stephen Leacock. To me he was the most amusing man who ever lifted a pen. I still think so. His book, *Sunshine Sketches of a Little Town,* is one of the warmest, funniest, and most devastating books ever written in Canada.

Pauline Johnson, who cried out passionately of the wrongs done the Indians by the white men, was herself the daughter of a Mohawk chief and an English mother. She could be soft, too. Step into a canoe and the gentle rhythm of "The Song My Paddle Sings" floats through your thoughts as a lovely undertone.

Later it was Hugh MacLennan and his fine book *Two Solitudes* that helped me to a better understanding of the conflict between the races in Quebec.

Farley Mowat, with his book, *People of the Deer,* and its sequels, has made Canadians—and people everywhere—aware of the plight of the Eskimos living west of Hudson Bay. Later, he had us all laughing with him in his hilarious book of boyhood memories, *The Dog Who Wouldn't Be.*

One of the many French-Canadian writers, Gabrielle Roy, has won international recognition with her novels about life in Quebec. The best known of these, *The Tin Flute,* won the Prix Femina in 1947.

For some reason, Canada has produced no famous playwrights. The best known is the French-Canadian, Gratien Gélinas, whose play *Ti-Coq* delighted Canadians but baffled New York audiences when he took it to Broadway.

Canadian painters have had a great influence on landscape painting everywhere. For many years our artists—English, Irish, Scottish, French, or whatever—painted pretty pictures of trees, lakes, and mountains in the old style. But gradually the bigness and brightness of the Canadian landscape had their effect. Painters began to use a boldness of design and color which at first horrified critics. This trend reached its peak with the Group of Seven, who spent much of their time living in tents and painting the rugged beauty of the Canadian Shield.

A culture development of greatest importance was the establishment by the Federal government in 1936 of the Canadian Broadcasting Corporation, which extended broadcasting to the remotest corners of Canada. It did more. It provided a theater where Canadian directors, actors, musicians, and writers could develop their art. As a result some of the most exciting radio drama on the continent was produced in Canada during the nineteen forties and early fifties. When television came the CBC extended its operations. Today it produces the type of fine show that is least often seen on commercial television—classical drama, ballet, opera, theater of the absurd.

In the field of public service the CBC's contributions are even more significant. The School Broadcast and Youth Programming Department provides the highest quality radio and television broadcasts, both for the classroom and the leisure hours. So Canadian students see productions of *Hamlet* or historical dramas or shows on nature science and others that could not be produced in the classroom.

The CBC's main function is to keep the people informed and its news broadcasts and public affairs shows, which cover anything that is going on anywhere, have become famous.

Although commercial movies have been slow to develop in Canada, many Canadian film actors have done well elsewhere. Among these are Mary Pickford, Norma Shearer, Raymond Massey, Lorne Greene, and Robert Goulet.

The National Film Board of Canada, also state supported, produces high-quality documentary films for showing in theaters, schools, and on television. Here, as with the CBC, worthiness of theme and production, rather than commercial value, is the chief criterion.

A great boost to the development of a distinctive Canadian culture was the establishment in 1957 of the Canada Council. With an original endowment of $50 million and with funds from other sources, the Council supports the arts and artists in Canada. Grants are given to dozens of worthy groups, such as the National Ballet of Canada, the Neptune Theatre Foundation in Halifax, Canadian Opera Company, Dominion Drama Festival, as well as to hundreds of individual students, painters, writers, musicians, social scientists, and others studying or doing research in Canada or abroad.

# 9

# What of the Future?

In 1967, Canada celebrated the one hundredth anniversary of confederation. During this centennial birthday party, lasting a full year, Canadians shed much of their usual conservatism, and set out to demonstrate to themselves—and to the world—that theirs was indeed a big, robust, potentially influential country.

Every city, town, and village had its centennial project—a new library, community center, park, or something else of permanent benefit. Through Festival Canada, Canadians everywhere were exposed to more concerts, plays, operas, ballets, films, pageants, circuses, sporting events, and art exhibitions than ever before. The World's Fair—Expo 67—in Montreal brought Canada into world focus.

But what of Canada's future? What are her chances of having a large population and becoming a great country?

First of all, until recently, Canada's development has been restricted by her harsh climate. Twenty-five years ago, for instance, nobody dreamed of building a city in the Arctic. Not so today. Man has gained so much control of his environment that life in the frigid Arctic can be as comfortable as life in balmy Florida. Whole communities can be covered by huge plastic domes under which the temperature, humidity, and winds can be set just as people like them. And the resources for hydroelectric and atomic power are at hand to do the job.

The great mineral wealth of the North will surely attract thousands of hardy people. Besides, it is known that much agriculture and ranching are possible on the vast plains of the Northwest Territories. New types of crops, better fertilizers, greatly improved machinery, more scientific methods can make the tundra into a garden.

Considering that the world is becoming overpopulated, it is entirely likely that this wide two-thirds of Canada, which is relatively unused

*The 25,000-seat Canadian Centennial Expo '67 Stadium in Montreal, scene of spectaculars and contests of all kinds, from military tattoos to sports.*

at the present, will support millions of people.

Thousands of immigrants from crowded countries come to Canada every year, and there is no doubt that many, many more will come in the future. They will bring with them, as they have in the past, their skills, their traditions, their energies, and their keen desire to build a good life.

And Canada is the land for the good life. She has, besides her boundless natural resources, a stable, democratic form of government by which each man is constitutionally equal to his neighbor. She has deeprooted traditions of justice and fair play. She has robust, resourceful people—a mixture of almost every race on earth—and a history of steady progress.

Canada is—in the truest sense—an emerging nation, with many surprises to offer.

# Index

## MAX BRAITHWAITE

was born in the prairie town of Nokomis, Saskatchewan, Canada, where, he says, "the land is flat as a table top and the wheat high as your belt." He lived in Prince Albert, Saskatchewan, and Saskatoon, where he attended the provincial normal school and the University of Saskatchewan. His book, *Why Shoot the Teacher?*, describes with good humor his first six months as a teacher in a desolate one-room prairie school set among the Russian thistle and grasshoppers.

After eight years of teaching and four in the Royal Canadian Navy, he decided to become a full-time writer and moved to Ontario to be close to the markets. He has written articles for *Maclean's, Chatelaine, Weekend,* and most other Canadian magazines.

Perhaps his greatest success has been as a writer of radio and television scripts for the Canadian Broadcasting Corporation. These include plays, documentaries, and hundreds of shows for the CBC School Broadcast Department. On eight different occasions shows written by him have won awards at the Institute for Education by Radio-Television of the Ohio State University.

He has also written a number of juvenile novels. Mr. Braithwaite's favorite activities are traveling in Canada and the United States with his family (three girls, two boys), camping, swimming, and hiking.